C000178869

The purpose of this study guide is to provide supplemental educational material. It is not intended as a substitute or replacement of NW.

Published by SuperSummary, www.supersummary.com

ISBN – 9798615499999

For more information or to learn about our complete library of study guides, please visit http://www.supersummary.com

Please submit any comments, corrections, or questions to: http://www.supersummary.com/support/

TABLE OF CONTENTS

British author Zadie Smith's tragicomic novel *NW* (Penguin Press, 2012), nominated for the Women's Prize for Fiction in 2013, presents the interconnected story of several protagonists living in contemporary London. The friendship of Leah Hanwell and Keisha (later Natalie) Blake is central to the narrative. As they grow from childhood, through adolescence, and adulthood, the two are repeatedly challenged in their attempts to navigate issues of social class, race, gender, education, career aspirations, and family life. Alongside their story, *NW* provides a glimpse into the life of Felix Cooper, who is struggling but determined to leave behind a life of addiction and self-destructive behavior. Though their identities and concerns may differ, the characters are united by their search for an authentic sense of self. The title of the novel refers to the postal code for the northwest region of the city, where all the characters live, and the geography of London shapes the lives and behavior of the characters as they attempt to define themselves.

Plot Summary

The novel's first part, "Visitation," centers on Leah's story. Born into a middle-class family of Irish immigrants, Leah enjoys a stable childhood in the Caldwell section of northwest London. She becomes best friends with Keisha at a young age, though the two develop distinct personalities and life trajectories. Leah marries a French Algerian immigrant, Michel. He is driven to climb the socio-economic ladder and start a family, while Leah becomes listless, secretly has an abortion, and covertly takes birth control. After a drug addict, Shar, cons her into giving her money, Leah becomes obsessed with tracking down and helping Shar, and she succumbs to a nervous breakdown.

The second part, "Guest," shifts to the story of Felix, who also grows up in Caldwell. Instead of pursuing an education and steady career like Leah and Natalie, he struggles with drug addiction for years. Eventually, he falls in love with Grace, who encourages him to turn his life around. He gets sober, breaks ties with his past, and focuses on improvement. Just as he reaches this turning point, however, he is mugged and killed by two men after a senseless argument on a train. The other principal characters of the novel learn about this murder via the news.

"Host," *NW*'s third part, dives deeper into the world of Keisha. Keisha is the daughter of working-class Jamaican immigrants, and her roots are humbler than Leah's. Nevertheless, she excels academically, transforms herself, and changes her name to Natalie in college. Along the way, she meets (then marries) a higher-class Italian immigrant, Francesco (Frank) De Angelis. Natalie becomes a successful lawyer and has two children. Despite her successes, Natalie remains unfulfilled and begins pursuing casual sex with strangers. When Frank discovers her secret life, their marriage, and Natalie's world, seem on the brink of collapse.

In the fourth part, "Crossing," a distraught Natalie flees home to wander the streets of Caldwell. She runs into one of her old schoolmates, Nathan Bogle, who is now a drug dealer and possible pimp. On the run himself, Nathan talks with Natalie about their past and present struggles. After contemplating suicide on a bridge, Natalie leaves Nathan behind and returns home. In the final part, also called "Visitation," Natalie and Frank attempt to navigate a marriage on the rocks. A frantic Michel, having discovered Leah's hidden birth control, calls Natalie for help, and Natalie visits her friend's home. She talks Leah out of her

3

nervous breakdown. In the aftermath, they realize that Felix's murderer might be Nathan, and they tip off the police.

The novel moves between first- and third-person perspectives and features flashbacks and side steps that complicate and enrich the narrative. *NW* is also experimental in style, including lists, records of instant message chats, stream-of-consciousness passages, and map directions as well as narrative. In resisting a straightforward plot, *NW* instead focuses on its characters' attempts to define themselves in the face of life events, both mundane and extreme. Set against the backdrop of diverse, complex London, *NW* provides a detailed impression of the chaos, confusion, and anxieties of modern urban existence.

Part 1, Pages 3-63

Part 1: "Visitation"

Part 1, Pages 3-22 Summary

NW begins at the home of 35-year-old Leah Hanwell, who is outside reading a magazine in her hammock. Thoughts of global warming, the heat, and the noise of her neighbors distract her. Her doorbell rings. Leah greets a frantic stranger, Shar, who asks for help for her mother, whom she says is in the hospital. Leah invites her in and then vaguely recognizes her as a classmate from long ago, when she attended the Brayton school.

They sit and drink tea as Shar tells a convoluted story. She says she has an abusive but absent husband and three kids, but she is unable to even remember the name of the hospital where she says her mother is. While Shar's story doesn't quite add up, Leah is nevertheless moved, intimately revealing that she found out that she is pregnant that morning. She tells Shar she does administrative work at an organization that distributes lottery money to charities and nonprofits. Leah goes to her bathroom to get money for Shar's cab ride to the hospital, sits on the floor, and cries. The doorbell rings; there is a driver at the gate outside. Leah's husband, Michel, a hairdresser, arrives. Leah gives £30 to Shar, who promises to return and pay Leah back before leaving with the car.

Shar does not return to pay Leah back, and it dawns on Leah that she has been conned. Leah talks with her mother, Pauline Hanwell, about what happened. Pauline assumes Shar is a drug addict and lectures Leah about being ripped off. Pauline seems to mistrust Michel but speaks with him on the phone about what happened, while Leah goes out to the yard and smokes marijuana with her stoner neighbor Ned.

Part 1, Pages 23-63 Summary

While out to buy croissants, Leah and Michel discuss Leah's age and their difficulty conceiving. In the pastry shop, they spot Shar. The trio struggles, but Shar runs out the door.

Leah muses about her physical attraction to Michel. She finds him stunningly beautiful and kind but thinks herself less beautiful. Leah had an abortion early in their relationship, before they were married, and is generally ambivalent about having children. Michel, however, wants to be "military about it" and have Leah become pregnant as soon as possible (28).

While Michel professes his desire to get ahead in life and to climb the corporate ladder, Leah does not find her work at the charity agency fulfilling, and the workplace itself is decrepit. She feels distant from her coworkers, who, although they think Michel is wonderful, allude to having issues with their mixed-race marriage.

Leah walks the streets of the NW district. En route, Leah sees Shar again. They shout back and forth before parting ways. Leah becomes obsessed with finding Shar, a pursuit she says seems more real to her than her slight baby bump. She learns that Shar is squatting in an apartment numbered 37, a number Leah is superstitious about.

Michel develops his own obsession, profiting from currency trading. While he spends time on their laptop trading, Leah sits outside smoking with Nate and thinks about her surprising admiration for him, about her father, and about the fact that Michel is trading using her inheritance from her father.

Later, Leah walks through the neighborhood and muses on its literary past. She sees Shar once again, this time grabbing her. Shar admits that she is a penniless addict and suggests that Leah should not be surprised about what happened. Leah, in turn, offers to get Shar help, which Shar refuses. Later, Leah pushes some addiction recovery brochures through the mail slot of apartment 37.

Part 1, Pages 3-63 Analysis

In the first sections of *NW*, readers confront Leah's experience with crime, marriage, pregnancy, and professional life. She represents a kind of ethical consciousness on one hand and near-emptiness on the other. The first scene presents her outdoors, surrounded by the literal and figurative noise of everyday life. She hears neighbors screaming and radio sounds, reads a magazine, and can't help but find her thoughts distracted by "world events and property and film and music [...] also sport and the short descriptions of the dead" (4). Readers do not find out much about Leah herself—her husband's name (Michel) even appears pages before her own. Though she has a job, a husband, and a home, and received an education, she struggles to find meaning, asking herself "what was the purpose of preparing for a life never intended for her?" (36).

Michel, on the other hand, is ambitious, "always moving forward, thinking of the next thing" (32). For him, this means increasing their income (through his currency trading scheme), eventually moving out of their modest apartment, and most importantly, having children. His optimism causes Leah to note, "Michel is a good man, full of hope. Sometimes hope is exhausting" (32). Despite their differences, Michel and Leah are united in being outsiders in some sense. Both are children of immigrants: Leah's mother is from Ireland, while Michel's family is French-Algerian. Both are uncomfortable in their current state of life, albeit for different reasons: Michel wants to climb the socio-economic ladder, while Leah wants to find her sense of self.

A range of external factors—economic, social, cultural—exacerbate their sense of alienation, threatening to disrupt life as they know it. The most immediate threat in this first section is the presence of criminal activity, represented by Shar. At the same time, Shar's entrance into Leah's life fills her existential void, at least temporarily. Leah has a soft spot for pitiful people—she works at an organization that distributes lottery money to charities and as a youth made a habit of talking to every homeless person she met. Thus, when Shar presents herself as a desperate woman in need instead of a drug addict, Leah can't help but try to help. Later, after Leah realizes that Shar had simply conned her, she becomes obsessed. The extent of the obsession is made clear by the episode in which she tracks down Shar's apartment and pushes addiction recovery leaflets through her mail slot. It is as though the drama Shar brought, no matter how deplorable, injected some much-needed life into Leah.

The geography of NW—eminently walkable—enables Leah's search for Shar, which itself represents her inner yearnings. Some passages in this first section of *NW* literally present her walking paths as directions from a navigation app. Others suggest them via a dizzying array of advertising snippets, sights, sounds, and smells: "TV cable, computer cable, audiovisual cables, I give you good price, good price. Leaflets, call abroad 4 less, learn English, eyebrow wax, Falun Gong, have you accepted Jesus as your personal call plan? Everybody loves fried chicken" (42). Elsewhere, this modern-day geography clashes with London's historical and literary past: The 19th-century novelist Charles Dickens is imagined to be walking "this far west and north for a pint or to bury someone. Look, there, on the library carpet between Science Fiction and Local History: a knotted condom filled with sperm. Once this was all farm and field with country villas" (60).

Passages like these exemplify the narrative voice of *NW*. The novel is experimental, showcasing a mix of styles that encompasses straightforward narrative, stream of consciousness, map directions, instant messaging chats, and more. The narrator, where there is one, is a third-person limited voice who does not give readers full insight into what characters are doing or thinking. *NW* is more interested in showing than explaining.

Part 1, Pages 64-109

Part 1, Pages 64-89 Summary

Leah arrives at an abortion clinic after hoping to find an old wives' method that works. While there, she reflects on her earlier abortions and the female lovers she had in the past. Though she finds the process of getting the abortion relatively painless, she feels "ashamed before an imagined nobody who isn't real and yet monitors our thoughts" (65).

Leah and Michel visit their friends Frank and Natalie (whose birth name is Keisha Blake) De Angelis, a barrister and a banker. Natalie and Leah reminisce about old Brayton schoolmates, trying to pin down who exactly Shar was. Michel interjects to say that Shar and her companions are probably addicts and pimps. From there, the conversation shifts to more mundane themes: children, boarding school, Michel's day trading. Leah catches Michel looking longingly at one of Frank and Natalie's kids.

Natalie has been looking for a church to get her kids into so that they can eventually enroll in a quality school. Leah accompanies her to look at one Pauline suggested, a country church in a decrepit neighborhood. Leah and Natalie stop to look at the old tombstones, musing on the past. Leah faints and then recovers in the company of her mother. While Leah reflects on her mother's nagging, someone calls and tells Leah to stop bothering Shar. Leah thinks the voice belongs to an old schoolmate, Nathan Bogle. Michel becomes upset at the caller's threat, and his reaction makes Leah surprisingly happy.

Part 1, Pages 90-109 Summary

Michel and Leah walk down a street and see someone they think is Nathan. Michel shouts at him, and the man pushes him. Leah then says it is not Nathan after all and begs the man not to attack them, claiming to be pregnant. The man kicks their dog, Olive, then leaves. Michel and Leah stagger home. At a dinner party at the home of Natalie and Frank, they discuss what happened as well as family life, raising children, and wanting to give them the best. Leah and Michel feel awkward around Natalie and Frank's friends. The built-up stress of this uneasiness causes them to have an argument, though they quickly make up.

The next morning, they discover that Olive is dead. This intensifies their worries. In mourning, Leah begins attending church every day to cope. Meanwhile, Michel continues with his plans to get ahead in life and puts them on a fertility waiting list to "go forward," though Leah secretly takes birth control.

They head to the home a friend of Frank's to celebrate carnival. At the party, they overhear that a 32-year-old man, Felix Cooper, was fatally stabbed in their neighborhood, on Albert Road. Michel tells Leah that he wants to move; she does not. Leah notes that Frank and Natalie, who are also at the party, seem to barely notice each other.

Leah goes to a store to retrieve photographs she had developed. The store clerk has trouble finding them at first. When Leah finally sees the pictures, she swears she sees Shar in some of them and becomes hysterical.

Part 1, Pages 64-109 Analysis

Leah, who mentions her pregnancy to Shar but not even Michel, decides to get an abortion. Initially ignorant, he discovers how Leah misled him by the end of the novel. This episode demonstrates the stark contrasts between Leah and Michel and their inability to reconcile their incompatible versions of what they want from life.

This section introduces Leah's friend Natalie and her husband, Frank. Later parts of *NW* detail the long, complex relationship between Natalie and Leah. The take-away from the first interaction between the two couples, however, is the stark class and professional contrast between them. While Leah and Michel work modest jobs at a non-profit and hairdresser's, Natalie and Frank are a successful barrister and banker, respectively. While Leah flounders to find meaning in life and Michel yearns to get ahead, Natalie and Frank apparently have made it, looking "like a king and queen in profile on an ancient coin," in Natalie's mind (67). Later, it becomes clear that Natalie and Frank have their own serious issues. In "Visitation," their problems are foreshadowed only at the carnival party, when Leah notices that Frank and Natalie hardly interact.

The external threats that were hinted at in the first sections of "Visitation" become physically realized in its second half. After verbal threats from Shar and a mysterious caller, and then the attack on Olive, the narrator notes that it "could be said that one of Michel's dreams has come true: they have gone up one rung, at least in the quality and elaboration of their fear" (102).

Several weeks later, Michel and Leah learn of the fatal stabbing of Felix Cooper. This turns out to be Felix, who is introduced in Part 2 of *NW*, and the incident is revisited from several perspectives throughout the novel. The initial conflict of the novel—Shar's theft of Leah's money—occurred in private space, after Leah invited her into her apartment. As the drama and violence heighten, they increasingly take place in the wider, public space of northwest London: first the attack on Olive, then the murder of Felix. This shift corresponds to a gradual pull to see seemingly private, domestic problems like those that Leah faces as systemic, social issues.

In "Visitation," the impact of the violence remains localized in the breakdown it precipitates in Leah. She mourns the death of Olive powerfully, and the fleeting spark of life brought on by the drama of Shar and the pride Leah felt at Michel defending her during the street attack quickly fades. The fracture between her and Michel continues to grow—he thinks they are trying to get pregnant, while she secretly takes birth control. The tipping point for Leah is when she discovers pictures of Shar mixed in with her own. Although readers are not shown the full extent of Leah's subsequent breakdown until Part 5 (also called "Visitation"), the improbable fact that Shar's photos were mixed in with hers hints at her mental instability. The narrator comments that the coincidence "[s]ounds reasonable but she can't take it reasonably" (108).

The incident shows that the issues and pressures Leah and others face—marriage, family, children, crime, class, society, work, ambition—have a powerful impact on mental health. *NW* depicts London as chaotic, dizzying, and stressful, regardless of its ostensibly high standard of living and international stature. This sense of chaos is reflected in the novel's stylistic experimentations, which continue throughout "Visitation." *NW* could be compared to works like James Joyce's classic *Ulysses,* which similarly utilizes a mix of experimental styles and genres and celebrates the geography of a world-famous city (Dublin). On the other hand, *NW* is contemporary in its themes, and its structure could reflect the confusion and conflicts of modern life even as it gives a nod to the tradition of literary experimentalism.

Part 2, Pages 114-154

Part 2: "Guest"

Part 2, Pages 114-154 Summary

Felix Cooper and his girlfriend, Grace, wake up and talk about small things, like a mermaid from Grace's collection of princess figurines that has fallen from a shelf. Grace bothers Felix, who works part-time, about not having made a "list of things he wanted from the universe" (115). She leaves, and Felix goes to see his father, Lloyd. When he arrives at Lloyd's messy, decrepit home, he is offered marijuana but refuses (135). Felix has brought Lloyd a book about the Garvey House, a housing project where Lloyd lived when he was younger. They reminisce about old times, and on page 37, they find a picture of Lloyd. On his way out, Felix runs into Lloyd's neighbor, Phil Barnes, who talks about how complicated families are and about how important nature is.

There is a brief flashback to when Grace and Felix first met, at a bus stop, which clarifies that he had a drug problem and is now recovering.

Felix meets a man, Tom Mercer, and they go to look at an old, damaged MG Midget that Tom is selling. On the way, they talk about Felix's past work in the film industry and Tom's marketing job. They head to a pub to talk the deal over. The conversation covers several topics, including Felix's two kids from an earlier marriage, and again turns to work. Felix has had all sorts of jobs, including running a failed T-shirt business. At the pub, Felix orders a ginger beer, to Tom's surprise, and he admits to being an alcoholic and to having been "deep in the drug thing" (146). At one point, Tom—who is hung-over—nevertheless asks Felix for drugs. Felix talks the price of the MG down to £450, despite Tom saying that his father would never let up if he sold the car for less than 700.

Part 2, Pages 114-154 Analysis

"Guest" presents a perspective distinct from the rest of the novel. While the other parts focus on Leah, Natalie, and their circle, Part 2 sheds light on the parallel story of Felix and his own London world. He invites comparisons to Leah, Natalie, and their circle. Like practically all of them, he has immigrant roots (his father is Jamaican). As a couple, Grace and Felix are like an inverse of Leah and

Michel: Grace's cheeriness and ambition echo Michel's, while Felix's not-immediately-visible dark past echoes the conflict that surges beneath Leah's seemingly placid surface (115).

The touching interactions between Felix and Lloyd serve to suggest the complexity of family relationships. Lloyd chides Felix for pursuing women who are a "black hole," drawing on his fractured relationship with Felix's mother, Jackie (126). Yet Lloyd is also a key to the layers of time captured on London's streets. The book of photos of the Garvey House that Felix brings to Lloyd shows pictures they reminisce over, including of Lloyd himself. This act literalizes the fact Felix and his family have a meaningful story, even if they might otherwise just seem like de-individualized parts of the London landscape. Felix's interaction with Lloyd's old friend and neighbor, Barnes, echoes this idea. He acknowledges both that families are complicated and that "I believe in the people, you see, Felix, I believe in them. Not that it's done me any good, but I do. I really do" (133). Felix's story is all the more authentic because of its conflict, including his own dysfunctional relationship with his distant mother and the drug addiction he has chosen to leave behind.

Perhaps influenced by Grace's optimism, Felix's story involves attempts to get ahead, much like Michel's. His savvy dealings with Tom over the sale of the MG he wants to buy for Grace are one example, and his multiple jobs and growing ambitions to get involved in the film industry are others. Tom serves as a foil to Felix's ambition. In keeping with the novel's exploration of the link between geography and human behavior, it is no surprise that a conversation about who Felix and Tom really are takes place as they walk through the streets of London, on the way to inspect the MG. Though Tom outwardly seems a picture of success—with a stable job, home, and girlfriend—he harbors feelings of inadequacy and "twenty-first century intellectual ennui" and senses that he is an "EPIC FAIL" in his parents' eyes (153, 152). With his crippling ennui despite an ostensibly controlled exterior, Tom recalls the character of Leah. This similarity connects "Guest" to the other parts of *NW*.

In terms of narrative structure, "Guest" presents an unusual situation. It is already known that Felix is dead, based on what is mentioned in "Visitation." With this spoiler willingly given, "Guest" takes the opportunity to tell Felix's backstory. Rather than remaining a faceless victim, he is shown to have a full-fledged past and set of personal conflicts and ambitions, just like other characters. By essentially interrupting the main plot of *NW* to present this additional story, the novel resists becoming a story about a murder. Instead, it becomes a novel about the conflicts of representative Londoners, including one who has been murdered.

Part 2, Pages 155-198

Part 2, Pages 155-198 Summary

Leaving the pub, Felix daydreams about science fiction and how the future seems to have come true. He heads to the messy apartment of his on-again-off-again lover, Annie Bedford. Annie is in the bath. They chat for a bit, then Felix reaches under the bath and pulls out a mirror with lines of white powder on it, then puts it back. Despite the decrepit appearance of her home and her obvious drug abuse, Annie is related to an earl who owns the land the apartment building sits on. Someone arrives at Annie's door. While she steps out of the bath to see who it is, Felix riffles through her medicine cabinet, examining the pills it contains.

The stranger at the door says he has attempted to contact Annie about signing an agreement for the building residents to split costs to improve the common areas. Annie becomes confrontational, but Felix tells the man to leave, promising that Annie will sign the agreement. Reflecting on the stranger at the door, her connection to the earl, and her lifestyle, Annie declares, "It happens that in this matter of property and drugs I am strong and they are weak. In other matters it's the other way around. The weak should take advantage of the strong, don't you think?" (172). She convinces Felix to stay a while, and they head to the roof.

Felix and Annie watch a family on the terrace of the building across the street. Felix tells Annie that his relationship with Grace is serious, even though they both previously had other lovers. He talks to Annie about how he's working hard to turn his life around and suggests she do the same: "I'm talking about what are your goals? What do you want for your life to be like?" (180). Annie retorts "Felix [...] I'm quite bored of talking now and personally I'd really like to know: are we going to fuck today or not?" (181). Immediately afterwards, Annie and Felix have sex. The two then argue about their diverging life paths. Felix says the relationship is over and leaves feeing lighter, while Annie collapses on the floor, sobbing.

Felix gets on a train and notices a missed call on his phone. He wonders if his brother, Devon, has called him from prison, which prompts him to reflect on memories of being with Devon and his mother, Jackie. At one point, Jackie returned to visit her sons. She quickly left, however, though not before stealing from them. Shortly afterwards, Devon robbed a jewelry store.

In the midst of this reverie, a pregnant woman on the tube asks Felix if his "friend" (actually a stranger on the other side) can move his feet so she can sit down. The woman assumes that the men are friends, since they are both black. Felix does not contest this but simply asks the man to move. The man and his companion argue with Felix. He gives up his own seat, feeling alternate waves of approval and contempt from the woman and men, respectively. Felix nevertheless exits the train in a good mood and jokes with some acquaintances he passes on the street. As Felix nears home, the two men he argued with on the train mug and then stab him. As Felix lies bloody on the sidewalk, he sees Grace just down the street, getting on her bus.

Part 2, Pages 155-198 Analysis

The second half of "Guest" seems almost an inverse of the first: Instead of offering a rosy depiction of Felix's ambitions and life with Grace, the section shows his darker side. Annie is a link to Felix's past drug use and failure to find direction in life. This is underscored in the brief rekindling of Felix's and Annie's romance when they have sex. It suggests a relationship that is fleeting and volatile, in contrast to the domestic stability he treasures with Grace. *NW* also makes this contrast clear in its references to space and material objects. In the opening pages of "Guest," Felix helps Grace retrieve a mermaid figurine that has fallen behind their bed, one of many (presumably Disney) figurines that Grace collects. The sunny optimism represented by the figurines is markedly different from the junk covering the residences of Lloyd and Annie, emphasizing the contrast between Felix's present and past. While Felix's visit to Lloyd builds bridges to his past (through a perusal of the Garvey House book), his motivation for visiting Annie is to say a final goodbye to the undesirable parts of his past—"demons," as he calls them—that she represents.

The impact of Felix's desire to get ahead in life, including his recovery from addiction, is most drastically indicated in his interactions with Annie. However, she is no simple representation of the London underbelly that Felix now wants to distance himself from. While some characters in *NW* have lives that are ostensibly successful and well put together but belie humble or dark pasts, Annie's is the opposite: She and her apartment appear decrepit and low-class, but her roots are high-class. As she mentions, she is related to an earl who owns the building she lives in as well as others that surround it. In its own way, this information signals a message that runs throughout *NW*: Urban life is not always what it appears to be.

Annie is markedly distinct from almost every other character in *NW*. While for Leah, Natalie, Michel, and many others, the clash between the material/social/economic aspects of urban life and the more existential ones causes anxiety, depression, and insecurity, Annie remains content with her life choices and the "river of fire" she lives in (185). Annie's jabs at the bourgeois couple on the rooftop across the street from her flat are not simply a reflection of her choice to lead a very different kind of life. Instead, they raise serious questions about Felix and Grace's own domestic ambitions. Annie is not afraid to take these questions to Felix directly, mocking his "pathological need [...] to be the good guy" (186). Clues about Annie's own history and complexity invite Felix to confront the purpose he has laid out for himself in a very serious way.

 Having already shown that the domestic life of at least two other representative Londoners—Leah and Michel—is far from bliss, *NW* presents these questions more broadly in "Guest." If Leah and Michel seemingly have all the right pieces in place yet happiness and purpose elude them, then it is unclear whether Annie or others are more authentic and true. Ultimately, all characters in *NW* struggle in some way or another to define purpose, meaning, and life trajectory in the complex and chaotic world of contemporary London.

After defining Felix as a person with a full and rich story, "Guest" closes with the shock of his murder. As in "Visitation," the act of violence happens on the streets of London, rather than in its private, domestic spaces, as if to bring the turmoil of life hidden beneath the cosmopolitan, urban veneer fully out into the open. The impact of the event is exacerbated by the fact that the newly liberated Felix happily declares himself in love to friends he passes just before being stabbed. The violent act echoes the attack on Leah, Michel, and Olive in "Visitation." It is also the link that joins the disparate strands of *NW* together by the novel's end, when Natalie and Leah realize they suspect who committed the murder: Nathan Bogle.

After the shock of the stabbing, "Guest" ends abruptly, with Felix taking his final breaths, watching Grace get on a bus and depart their neighborhood—and symbolically, the violence and drama it represents. "Guest" sheds the literary experimentalism of the other sections of *NW*. It is essentially a self-contained and straightforward narrative, yet it contributes to a key aspect of the novel. By humanizing Felix, it gives the more extended stories of Leah and Natalie more depth. The links between the characters and parts show that their conflicts are not isolated but instead part of the broader fabric of contemporary London life.

Part 3, Pages 201-235

Part 3: "Host"

Part 3, Pages 201-212 Summary

The third part of *NW* begins with the story of how Keisha (later Natalie) Blake and Leah Hanwell meet and bond. One day when they are children, Keisha pulls the nearly drowned Leah from a pool. Consequently, Leah and Keisha become inseparable friends. "Host" tells their story through a series of short anecdotes and observations, some only a sentence long, that jump around from topic to topic.

Leah and Keisha have very similar likes and dislikes. However, Keisha's awareness of the class differences between the Blakes and the Hanwells grows. She sometimes envies or mimics her friend's family. When Leah visits her house, for instance, Keisha attempts to make tea the way the Hanwells do; yet when Keisha's father Augustus (Gus), a plumber, takes the two to McDonald's for lunch, they squeal with delight. On the walk back, they run into Pauline (a nurse studying to become a radiographer), who tells Leah she needs to go with her.

Keisha is intelligent and curious, once asking Leah's father, Colin Hanwell, what talk radio is, as she cannot fathom what it means to listen to something other than music on the radio. Leah and Keisha both enroll at Brayton Comprehensive. As Keisha's academic confidence grows, she marvels at Leah's burgeoning social consciousness and interests in areas like animal rights, poverty, and war.

Part 3, Pages 212-235 Summary

Keisha also becomes more aware of racial differences, with her family telling her "whatever you did in life you would have to do it twice as well as they did 'just to break even'" (213). As their broader interests and concerns begin to diverge, Leah and Keisha's friendship cools. Leah often accompanied Keisha and her family to Kilburn Pentecostal church, but one Sunday she tells Keisha she wants to see some friends in another neighborhood, Camden Lock, instead. She takes the number 37 bus to go there, and 37 becomes an unlucky number in Keisha's mind.

Leah and Keisha begin to explore more mature interests. Keisha looks older than she really is and is often asked to buy alcohol for Leah and other teens. On Keisha's 16th birthday, Leah buys her a vibrator. She begins using it frequently, and, given her natural intelligence and curiosity, she considers the concepts of masturbation and orgasm in a highly analytical way. Keisha's mother, Marcia, discovers the vibrator and deduces that it came from Leah. She enforces a year-and-a-half-long break between the friends, during which Keisha experiences extreme loneliness. Marcia sets Keisha up with Rodney Banks, a Caribbean youth from the same corridor, assuming that they will get along because they both like to read.

Keisha gives in and begins spending time with Rodney, reading literature, studying for exams, and planning for college. Marcia wants Keisha to enroll in a one-year business administration course at the nearby Coles Academy, but Keisha has her sights on schools farther away from home in Manchester and Edinburgh. The cost of traveling to these schools is prohibitively expensive for the

Blakes, however, so Keisha rules out many of them. She eventually runs into Leah at a community meeting, where they chat about school, and they resume contact. Both girls spend their last summer in NW, though the Hanwells have moved into a maisonette. Leah parties and hangs out in a park, while Keisha works in a bakery, going to the park only occasionally.

Part 3, Pages 201-235 Analysis

The backstory of Leah and Natalie/Keisha partially explains the conflicts that each face throughout *NW*, namely, their struggle to find purpose and meaning in their lives. On one hand, they grow close over shared experiences and likes—music, boys, school, play, time spent at each other's houses, and other essentially normal aspects of urban life. On the other hand, their distinct personalities are evident nearly from the start.

Keisha is intelligent, curious, and driven to succeed academically. She approaches the entire world with an analytical frame of mind, expressing this through everything from writing computer programs to a systematic discussion of the "charged question of clitoral versus vaginal orgasm" (222). While Leah is no failure, her motivations are less defined, and she is pulled more by a curiosity about people than about knowledge; as the narrator puts it, "no one ever mistook Keisha's cerebral willfulness for her friend's generosity of spirit" (210). This is nowhere more evident than when a mutual friend divulges to Leah and Keisha that her mother was raped by her cousin, who is thus her father. Keisha is rather unaffected, while the other two weep. In their later teen years, these distinct personalities play a part in the two friends' drifting apart. Though they reunite and continue their friendship, their differences are more openly evident than before.

NW makes clear that the differences between Keisha and Leah are not simply a matter of personality, however, but are more broadly indicative of London's socio-cultural diversity. Leah's white, English-Irish family is educated and professionalized. Keisha's family emigrated from Jamaica and is working-class. "Host" repeatedly emphasizes that family influences behavior. Leah's mother and father appear relatively hands-off, corresponding to their daughter's free and open spirit. Keisha's mother, Marcia, is far more controlling. She shows her ability to influence even the strong-willed and intelligent Keisha after discovering her vibrator, initiating the break between Leah and Keisha, and setting Keisha up with a boyfriend of Marcia's choosing, Rodney.

NW makes one of its geographically minded points by suggesting that the intersection of cultures that happens in Leah and Keisha's friendship is possible because of the diversity that exists in northwest London's cosmopolitan space, where residents with distinct cultures and identities live next to each other. At the same time, *NW* suggests another reality of this cosmopolitanism—some residents resist and flee this multiculturalism—when the Hanwells move out of the neighborhood. The impact of cultural and socio-economic differences is also illustrated by the lower-class Keisha's academic excellence yet limited college choices, for instance.

Stylistically, "Host" picks up where the literary experimentalism of "Visitation" left off. This part of the novel is composed of 184 sections—some as short as a sentence, others as long as a few pages—showcasing a wide range of genres and styles, including straightforward narratives, lists, directions, and aphorisms. It also evidences literary play. For example, Keisha decides that the number 37 is unlucky after Leah decides not to go with her to church one day and instead takes a bus of that number to visit friends in another area. In a subtle gesture, "Host" then omits a section numbered 37 and instead jumps from section 36 to section 38. By a strange coincidence, it is apartment number 37 that Shar lives in and Leah stops by in "Visitation" to deliver addiction recovery leaflets. The stylistic experimentation and rapid shifts of "Host" mimic the confusion, clash of social classes, and general unsettledness of London life.

Part 3, Pages 235-292

Part 3, Pages 235-247 Summary

Keisha attends Bristol with Rodney, where they spend time studying together, and they decide to pursue law. Outside of class, they socialize mainly with older people from a church they attend. Keisha feels alienated and notes that her fellow "students were tired of things Keisha had never heard of, and horrified by the only thing she knew well: the Bible" (235-236).

Leah and Keisha visit each other at school occasionally. Leah also feels alienated, asking herself "What am I doing here, with all these smart bastards? Has someone made a mistake somewhere?" (237). She hangs out with artistic types—her boyfriend makes films about boredom—and by her third visit, Keisha hardly recognizes Leah, who has grown dreadlocks and changed her style of clothing.

Keisha undergoes her own evolution, deciding to call herself Natalie. She becomes infatuated with a new classmate, Francesco (Frank) De Angelis, and bored with

Rodney. On her third visit, Leah spends the night with Bristol student Alice Nho while Natalie decides it is over with Rodney. She begins to casually date other men but really wants Frank.

Part 3, Pages 247-292 Summary

Natalie sheds her religious commitments, losing "God so smoothly and painlessly she had to wonder what she'd ever meant by the word" (247). At the same time, she develops new interest in things as diverse as activism and clubbing. She runs into Frank occasionally. At a dinner with fellow students and one of her professors, Frank drinks too much and makes controversial comments, including about the school's lack of diversity. He later apologizes to Natalie for his behavior, and they begin seeing each other.

Frank was born in Italy to a mixed-race couple (an Italian mother and a Trinidadian father) and comes from a higher class than Natalie. Explaining his background in his own words, he says, "Rare Negroid Italian has happy childhood, learns Latin, the end" (263). As they approach the end of their schooling, they become serious. Frank understands how important Leah is to Natalie and makes friends with her. Natalie enters pupillage, while Frank fails the bar exam and begins working at an investment company. Natalie's pupillage leaves her in a financially precarious state. She intends to use some money saved from childhood, but Marcia lent it to her pastor in some sort of scam. Frank's mother, Elena De Angelis, offers to give Natalie the money she needs.

Frank and Natalie get married, and Natalie begins practicing law. A defense attorney she works for, Johnnie Hampton-Rowe, molests her. Afterwards, she is mentored by another lawyer, Theodora Lewis-Lane, who advises

Natalie, "one learns very quickly in this profession, fortune favors the brave—but also the pragmatic" (284). She also tells Natalie, "I took some advice early on: 'Avoid ghetto work,'" arguing that Natalie will otherwise be viewed as aggressive and hysterical. Natalie nevertheless rents a flat in NW and takes a job at a small firm.

Part 3, Pages 235-292 Analysis

Leah and Keisha (now Natalie) rapidly develop in college and immediately afterwards. The inclination toward social consciousness that Leah displayed as a child transforms into full-fledged activism as she bonds with nonconformists at her college. While as a youth she experimented with drinking and other rebellious behavior, in college, she experiments with clubbing and club drugs. She also changes her physical appearance, adopting dreadlocks, for instance. Simultaneous with these social developments, the insecurity and disaffection that Leah felt as a child also grows, as she wonders why she is in college and if she even belongs. "Host" shows the first full articulation of Leah's existential questions, which reemerge later in her life.

Her best friend's transformations are no less significant. Upon arrival at college in Bristol together with Rodney, Keisha feels alienated from other students, whose social class and general concerns seem vastly different from her own. This feeling does not stop her from cutting ties with Rodney, her link to her past life in northwest London, signifying that her response to alienation is simply to become more determined and willfully self-confident. Keisha's adoption of a new name, Natalie, is an obvious indication of her attempt to find a new identity, even as she grapples with feelings of "having no self to be" (246). Natalie's distancing of herself from Rodney, London, and her old name come together with her interest in other men (most importantly, Frank) and her continued academic success.

This section of "Host" is distinct, as it contains the only parts of *NW* set outside of London. The distance from home that both Leah and Natalie are granted by attending their respective colleges affords them a cognitive separation from their past lives. Though they visit each other on a semi-regular basis, the two friends spend most of their time apart. This separation from home and from each other enables each young woman to develop her identity more fully—even if those identities turn out to be tentative and uncertain. Given that this development coincides with their education, this section of *NW* has affinities with the genre known as *Bildungsroman* or coming-of-age story (literally, the term is German for "novel of education").

Whereas a Bildungsroman would show a protagonist overcoming conflicts to emerge with a fully formed identity, however, Natalie struggles to define herself. This extends even to her relationship with Frank, the most important new figure in her life. Like Natalie, Frank has immigrant roots and is a minority (he is mixed-race), but his higher-class background causes Natalie to confront the reality that even shared racial or cultural identity does not prevent alienation. As a passage in "Host" sarcastically puts it, "Low-status person with intellectual capital but no surplus wealth seeks high-status person of substantial wealth for enjoyment of mutual advantages" (270). Frank's class standing and his mother make her uncomfortable, and she begrudgingly accepts money from her to fund her legal apprenticeship. Nevertheless, Natalie and Frank are united in their ambitiousness, making their eventual marriage seem almost inevitable.

Despite the major transformations that Natalie goes through during this period of her life away from home, by the end of this section, she decides to return to northwest London to live and work. Ultimately, Leah does as well, suggesting the powerful pull of the geography of home.

Part 3, Pages 292-355

Part 3, Pages 292-355 Summary

Natalie becomes absorbed in her work. At one point, when having brunch with some of her married friends, she realizes, "She could only justify herself to herself when she worked. If only she could go to the bathroom and spend the next hour alone with her email" (300). Yet she also begins to doubt her work doing "good deeds." She also begins to question her marriage and develops a habit of checking listings for people seeking sex, which she hides from Frank.

Natalie also seeks out her mother and siblings, with mixed results. In response to Cheryl's messy house and rambunctious kids, Natalie says she hates to see her sister living like this, prompting an argument. Yet when visiting her brother, Jayden, who has come out, she gets drunk with him and learns about his life and how proud he is of her. Natalie also casually runs into her old schoolmate Nathan. Though she is unsure of how to talk to him at that moment, she will have a later run-in with him in the fifth part of *NW*, "Crossing."

Frank and Natalie move into a new house in a more upscale area. Marcia pressures Natalie about not having children. She and Frank eventually have two children. She is uneasy in her role as a wife, mother, and professional success, however, and feels distant from her roots: "Natalie Blake had completely forgotten what it was like to be poor. It was a language she'd stopped being able to speak, or even to understand" (330). She feels uncomfortable seeing old acquaintances, like her friend Layla, who thinks she always wanted to seem above others. Even the sexual liaisons Natalie seeks all turn out to be unsatisfactory.

Her friendship with Leah continues throughout all of this time, however, though Natalie suspects that Leah is depressed, especially after Leah's run-in with Shar. Shortly afterwards, Frank discovers Natalie's secret life when he stumbles across her private email account, KeishaNW@gmail.com. They argue, and Frank asks Natalie, "Who are you?" before she leaves, saying she is going "[n]owhere."

Part 3, Pages 292-355 Analysis

Natalie and Frank catapult themselves into professional and family life at a frantic pace. In a superficial sense, both Natalie and Frank have "made it." The traditional pieces of urban/suburban domestic life fall into place for them one by one, as they enter their careers, acquire a home (then an even larger one), have children, and move up the socio-cultural-economic ladder. They appear to be success stories, a point most true for Natalie, given her humble roots. The couple represents, in this light, what characters like Felix and Michel aspire to achieve.

Right alongside their chain of successes, however, "Host" makes Natalie's existential crisis palpable. Career and family conflicts plague Natalie, for example. After avoiding having kids until seeming to cave in to pressure from Marcia to do so, Natalie remains uneasy with her children, reacting to them with "simple ambivalence." On some level, this may be attributed to the aloofness and emotional detachment that has defined her since childhood. More poignantly, however, Natalie's discomfort with juggling children and career directly points to a dilemma many women face in London and elsewhere. Even for a woman as academically, professionally, and economically successful and confident as Natalie, the challenges of having and raising children alongside a career can cause anxiety, depression, and other conflicts. Natalie's problem is not localized to her life but rather is indicative of a widespread issue in the world she inhabits.

Natalie's growing boredom also emerges as a major theme. Despite her successes and achievements, she remains unfulfilled. Natalie approaches her proposed solution to her problem of boredom—casual threesomes with strangers— with her distinctive matter-of-factness. She begins by checking and signing up with sites for people seeking sex and then proceeds to check out each lead one by one. Ironically, on each of these rendezvous, Natalie seems more interested in the strangers' houses and the objects in them than in the sex itself. This point suggests that the sex Natalie seeks is not ultimately what she yearns for, supported by the fact that none of the encounters leaves her satisfied.

As "Host" comes to a close and Frank discovers Natalie's secret sexual pursuits, this sense of yearning in the face of outward success moves front and center. As *NW* has already shown several times through characters like Leah and Frank, life in northwest London is not always what it appears to be, and disaffection touches everyone. While "Host" closes by bringing conflicts of identity and purpose into intimate, private spaces (Frank's and Natalie's home and bedroom), the final two sections of *NW* bring them back out into public, along with a reminder of how those conflicts intersect with the physical and human geography of London.

Part 4

Part 4: "Crossing"

Part 4 Summary

In a daze, Natalie walks through the streets of NW, up
Willesden Lane to Kilburn High Road. The road is blocked,
and police inform her that there has been some sort of
incident. Without aim or purpose, Natalie heads back to
Caldwell: "Walking was what she did now, walking was
what she was. She was nothing more or less than the
phenomenon of walking" (360). Someone calls for her, and
it turns out to be Nathan. He mentions she doesn't look
good and correctly guesses that she's been arguing with
Frank.

Nathan tells Natalie (Keisha, as he calls her), "It's either fly
or give it up tonight," and he urges her to come with him
(362). They walk through the streets. Nathan offers Natalie
marijuana laced with something harder. The drugs hit
Natalie hard; "She was as high as she'd ever been in her
life" (376). She wants to go into a cemetery. They watch a
fox, which they call a "sneaky animal." When they see the
lights of the police, however, they take off.

Wandering to a train station, Nathan tells Natalie to hold
back for a minute. She watches him score something off of
two girls, and then they continue walking toward a
gentrified area. While a helicopter circles above, Nathan
describes his woes to Natalie: "Had enough of this city. I'm
tired of it right now for real. Bad luck follows me, Keisha"
(376). He declares that for black males like him, life
becomes hard after age 10, when they are viewed no longer
as cute children but as threats to be judged. He then begins
to belittle the domestic troubles Natalie has been

experiencing. Offended, she starts to run away, trips, gets up, and continues with Nathan following.

They bicker. Recalling Leah's incident, Natalie confronts Nathan about one of the girls at the tube station: "Wasn't she at Brayton? She looked familiar to me. Is her name Shar?" (382). Natalie begins to wonder if Nathan is a pimp or has some other kind of power over the girls.

They finally approach a bridge on Hornsey Lane famed as a suicide spot. Natalie has an epiphany once she arrives, realizing she's subconsciously been heading to the bridge since leaving home. She notes that the bridge has spikes on its edges, which "must be how they stopped people going nowhere" (384). Though she stands on the bridge contemplating suicide, Natalie ultimately does not go through with it. Laughing, she leaves, though not fully grasping what compelled her to survive.

Part 4 Analysis

The fourth part of the novel places Natalie in a setting that by now seems both strange and entirely unnatural: back on the streets of northwest London. If in "Host," the narrator notes that Natalie has forgotten her roots and what it was like to be poor, in "Crossing," Natalie unavoidably confronts the poverty and geography of her youth. Wandering aimlessly through the space of her old stomping grounds in NW, Natalie also confronts the ghosts of her past, represented by Nathan. The outer contrasts between the two are stark: the successful lawyer, wife, and mother of two meets the criminal and possible pimp. Indirect evidence begins to mount that Nathan is involved in Felix's murder and is on the run from the police.

Paralleling how a reformed Felix's visit to Annie does not reduce Annie to a flat, weak caricature, Nathan's interactions with Natalie have him asking probing, serious questions about her life. Nathan may be a criminal and murderer, but he is also able to confront Natalie about the false facade of her life precisely because he wears his wrongdoings and mistakes openly, and precisely because he is connected to Natalie's roots: "I done some bad things Keisha I'm not gonna lie. But you know that ain't really me," he tells her, emphasizing, "You know me from back in the day" (366).

On the run from the police, Nathan also enables Natalie to escape from the structure of her life, physically (via their flight through the streets) and chemically (via the drugs Nathan supplies her with). In this moment, neither her "real" life nor her drug-fueled flight with Nathan can be said to be more authentic than the other. She is able to put her life and fate on pause, however, and "Crossing" similarly slows down the narrative of *NW* considerably. While "Host" comprises nearly 200 rapidly moving short sections stretching from Keisha's youth to Natalie's present day, time in "Crossing" is far less compressed. Its sections are named after roads and geographic locations in NW, emphasizing place over time.

Natalie's journey with Nathan through the London district is far from linear. Heading up Albert Road, she is blocked by an incident (Felix's murder scene). She then backtracks before heading to Caldwell, where she runs into Nathan. They move from location to location in the old neighborhood before winding up at the bridge on Hornsey Lane. The novel moves readers from place to place along with the characters, taking them along but not divulging where they are going or what they are doing. Distraught or at least shaken by her falling out with Frank, Natalie is on an aimless journey that matches the spiritual directionlessness she faces in life, the "nowhere" she told Frank she was heading toward as she left their home.

Indeed, it is only at the bridge that Natalie realizes she has subconsciously been heading there the entire evening. As Annie and Felix casually mention in "Guest," the site is famed as "Suicide Bridge" (169). Having thus foreshadowed the event, Natalie nearly goes through with the act but ultimately stops herself, feeling saved by an unnamed force. In the final part of *NW*, called "Visitation" like the first part, that something proves to be a pull toward the very spaces and people of home that Natalie has been trying to escape.

Part 5

Part 5: "Visitation"

Part 5 Summary

Back home, in their bedroom, Natalie has left a note of apology and/or explanation for Frank. He prepares to go out for the day, however, and leaves the letter unopened. Ruminating on the breakdown in their marriage and relationship, Natalie believes "[t]hat this was her life now. Two silent enemies shepherding children to their social appointments" (389). With Frank out, Natalie is left to handle their children on her own for the day. Uncomfortable with this in general and in particular given her marital discord, she decides to take them to carnival to keep them occupied.

She sees a newspaper headline mentioning a killing on Albert Road, near where Natalie was during her wanderings with Nathan. A picture in the story shows a

Rastafarian man holding a picture of his adult son. Natalie can read the name "Felix" from a picture within the picture, and she recognizes him as a resident of Caldwell, though she does not know him personally.

Michel calls Natalie, in great distress. He says that Leah seems to have shut down after being upset about photos she had developed at a pharmacy—the same ones that she believes show Shar. Michel also discovers the birth control pills that Leah has been taking, and that their package has Natalie's name on them. Given his strong desire to have children, he is angry with Natalie and demands an explanation. Worried about Leah, he also asks Natalie to come over.

At the apartment, Natalie leaves her children indoors and goes out to Leah, who refuses to speak. Finally, when Natalie's son, Spike, runs out to her, Leah tells her "You look like the fucking Madonna" (399). Distraught, Leah says "I just don't understand why I have this life" (399), to which Natalie responds, "Because we worked harder" (400). In the process of trying to encourage Leah by telling her how good she has it, Natalie realizes that at that moment, all she really wants is to be with Frank and talk to him. Natalie tells Leah she thinks she knows about what happened during the "incident" described in the newspaper, suspecting that Nathan is involved, and they tip off the police.

Part 5 Analysis

The fifth and final part of *NW* is titled "Visitation," just like its first part, yet the opening and closing of the novel are linked to each other by more than just their titles. The disparate strands of the novel are brought together: While the first part named the victim of the stabbing as Felix, the final part names the probable murderer as Nathan, thanks to the action of Natalie and Leah.

While Natalie has been keeping her marital and existential woes hidden up to this point in the novel, they are now unavoidably obvious. Leah and Michel's conflicting domestic ambitions also reemerge, this time openly. When Michel discovers the birth control pills Leah has secretly been taking, he at first thinks that they belong to Natalie (as they have her name on their package, since Leah had been stealing them from Natalie). Given his ambition to start a family, he is distraught at this discovery. Nevertheless, Michel begs Natalie to come to their home, signifying her importance for Leah. Ironically, Leah only stirs when she sees Natalie with her kids, albeit with the sarcastic statement, "You look like the fucking Madonna" (399).

Lost in their respective domestic and existential breakdowns, the two long-term friends find each other again. Despite all of the changes each has gone through, despite their diverging life paths, and despite their fundamental differences of background, identity, and perspective on life, they continue to relate to one another. In this moment of high drama, they are linked in the fact that each has essentially done something extreme to her husband—one hiding an abortion and lying about trying to become pregnant, the other hiding a secret life of affairs.

Their connection in the moment grows into something else. Most immediately, in their conversation in Leah's yard, they verbalize the questions about who they are, and what they live for, that each has been grappling with internally throughout the novel. Though their answers to the questions are tenuous, the very act of stating them reawakens a sense of life within each of them. As Leah begins to talk to Michel again, Natalie realizes that she longs to reconnect with Frank.

The two also connect over the incident of Felix's murder. When Natalie tells Leah she knows something about what happened, and they decide to do something about it, they act together. When the novel closes by stating, "Natalie dialed it. It was Keisha who did the talking" (401), this symbolizes Keisha's peeling back the layers of time and change to face her past with assurance and confidence, blending the present with the past instead of avoiding it.

The close of *NW* also brings attention back to one of its core themes—the relationship between the geography of northwest London and the behavior of the residents who live within it. Throughout the novel, Natalie, Leah, and others have come into conflict with the spaces and life of NW, attempting to leave it physically (for education, or better housing), socio-economically (by getting ahead in life or climbing the corporate ladder), or mentally-spiritually (through drug use, affairs, or mental breakdowns). The threats surrounding personal and domestic life—crime, violence, racism, existential crisis— are made clear in the novel. However, by choosing to tip off the police about Nathan Bogle's involvement in the murder of Felix Cooper, Natalie and Leah resolve to do something about at least one of these threats. By returning energy and effort to the world of northwest London, Natalie and Leah resolve themselves to accept it as a home of sorts, yet without ignoring or erasing all the shortcomings, crises, confusion, and chaos that it contains.

Leah Hanwell

While the plot of *NW* is built around the relationship between Leah and Keisha/Natalie, the first part of the novel is devoted to exploring Leah's perspective on the world. Outwardly, Leah's life looks put together, if not particularly exciting. Her modest but steady job helping distribute funds to charities suits her socially conscious personality, she finds her devoted husband Michel beautiful, and she has a stable network of family and friends in northwest London.

Inwardly, however, Leah's life is in turmoil. In particular, she feels constantly at odds with Michel's can-do attitude and desire to get ahead in life and start a family. Leah experiences an existential crisis, going through the motions of life more than being motivated by anything concrete. Though she believes in others, Leah is fundamentally unsure of herself.

Within the novel's plot, Leah's character sharpens Natalie's own set of existential issues and demonstrates how pervasive the challenges of life in NW are. The novel's attention to Leah and Natalie's backstory demonstrates that the crises of identity that the characters face are not simply a matter of adults feeling unhappy. Instead, they are an almost inescapable aspect of modern life, from childhood on.

Leah is a foil to Natalie, highlighting her friend's intelligence and professional ambition. At the same time, Leah's modest life makes her into a kind of everywoman, flawed and vulnerable, yet relatable. Thus, when Leah has a nervous breakdown, her crisis does not appear unusual but like one that could happen to anyone. In that moment, Leah's lifelong friend Natalie arrives to help her out of her situation, and as the novel ends, Leah and Natalie appear ready to approach their lives anew.

Keisha Blake/Natalie De Angelis

The bulk of *NW* presents the world through Natalie's eyes, although filtered by the lens of the limited narrator. Natalie is intelligent and driven, and nothing seems to stop her from succeeding in life—neither her humble roots, nor her race, nor her economic struggles, nor her controlling mother, nor an initially modest job, nor her first boyfriend (Rodney) or husband (Frank).

While seen as a paradigm of success, Natalie experiences alienation, disaffection, and a yearning for something unknown, just like her best friend, Leah. Though her academic and professional ambitions are constant, the struggles of identity and purpose that follow Natalie from childhood on contribute to her continual evolution. When Leah gives her a vibrator for her 16th birthday, for instance, Keisha/Natalie's latent sexuality blooms. When her mother forces her to avoid Leah for over a year, she becomes even more entrenched in her academic ambition to counter feelings of alienation. When given the opportunity to get away in college, she sheds her boyfriend Rodney, her religious beliefs, and even her given name. When she finds that her life as a successful barrister, wife, and mother are unsatisfying, she looks for fulfillment in casual threesomes with strangers.

The shifts Natalie goes through drive the novel's plot, until her near-collapse in "Crossing" and eventual desire to reunite with Frank and to tip off the police about Felix's murder provide some sense of an ending, however tenuous.

In each of these stages of development and change, Natalie searches for purpose and meaning, which elude her. The fact that she inwardly seems compelled to search for fulfillment while simultaneously upholding her domestic and professional life makes clear that the existential crises of modern life described throughout *NW* touch people at all positions on the socio-cultural-economic spectrum.

Michel

Whereas Leah and Natalie are propelled by struggles to find purpose and meaning, Leah's husband, Michel, is driven by the pursuit of material and social success. For Michel, the path to a meaningful life is clear. First, he wants to increase his income, supplementing his job as a hairdresser with attempts at profiting from currency trading. Second, the resulting economic success he envisions would enable him and Leah to leave their modest apartment and buy a more impressive home. Finally, Michel is insistent that he and Leah need to have children.

Though Michel represents the desire for success as defined in modern urban life, each of these ambitions is thwarted. Frank advises Michel to be wary of currency trading, Michel and Leah remain in their flat, and Leah's secret abortion and use of birth control prevent them from having children. By holding on to ambitions of success that elude him, Michel makes Leah's and Natalie's existential crises seem all the more pressing.

Michel does undergo his own evolution, however, at the moment of one of the book's most urgent crises. When Leah collapses mentally, Michel is upset about her lying to him about trying to become pregnant. Nevertheless, he sheds his economic and social ambitions to instead turn attention to the woman he loves, frantically asking Natalie,

"Why does she hate me?" and begging her to come help Leah recover (396). Significantly, it is while talking to Michel in his moment of pain, fear, and agony that Natalie first comes to reassess her life and walk back from her own near-breakdown.

Frank De Angelis

Like Michel, Frank is associated with economic and social success—the difference being that while Michel yearns for it, Frank seems to have attained it. Born in Italy to a white mother and a black father, Frank also represents the multiculturalism touched on throughout the novel, yet he is distinct from other characters with immigrant roots (especially Natalie, Michel, and Felix) because he was born into a relatively well-off family.

While professionally ambitious and educated like Natalie, Frank initially lacks seriousness. He becomes drunk at an important school dinner, for instance, and later fails the bar exam. He demonstrates an ability to bounce back from challenges and advances professionally as an investment banker. Ultimately, Frank transforms, settling into domesticity and fatherhood while, unbeknownst to him, Natalie pursues a secret life.

This contrast helps depict the extent of Natalie's crisis. The questions she faces—about motherhood, success, and happiness—appear even more urgent in the face of Frank's seemingly effortless acceptance of life. Frank, however, is hurt by the discovery of Natalie's secret, refusing to even accept a note of explanation from her. When Natalie experiences Michel's and Leah's pain during their own domestic crisis at the end of the novel, she begins to understand Frank's.

Felix Cooper

The story of Felix and those around him steps to the side of *NW*'s main narrative: These characters are the only ones not directly related to the main characters Leah and Natalie. Like the others, however, Felix represents northwest London. The novel makes this clear by concentrating on the qualities that he shares with other characters, including professional ambition, a domestic and personal past that is far from perfect (he has dealt with both drug addition and a broken home), immigrant roots, and the search for meaning.

Felix's rocky past and family, coupled with the influence of his plucky girlfriend, Grace, and his decision to turn his life around, provide him an authentic mix of optimism and realism. Just before his death, Felix is saying goodbye to the dark parts of his past, motivated by the desire to change and advance. At the same time, he is far from ignorant of the challenges that life can dish out.

The senseless murder of Felix is a key plot point in *NW*, linking its first and final parts and essentially wakening Leah and Natalie from their existential stupor. By devoting "Guest" to Felix, however, *NW* resists making him into a mere victim. Instead, it provides an opportunity to see the tragedy as a full, human story, joining other crises—like Leah and Natalie's ennui and Michel's attempts to get ahead—in the tableau of authentic challenges of London life.

The Relationship between Urban Geography and Human Behavior

NW declares its connection to geography in its very title, which refers to the actual postal code for northwest London. The novel makes numerous references to street names, bridges, parks, buildings, and map directions—most of which highlight real places. However, the novel is not simply interested in providing a realistic depiction of London. Rather, the geographic references are a backdrop against which characters' identities, motivations, and actions emerge.

On one hand, London spaces are imagined to define people. In section 173 of "Host," for instance, characters at a public pool are having an argument, each proudly mentioning where they are from with the implication that some areas of London (like Hackney) are superior to others (like Harlesden). On the other hand, the attempts of characters such as Natalie, Michel, and Leah to leave certain neighborhoods (with varying degrees of success) shows that a core conflict in the novel is the struggle against the idea that where a person is from defines who they are.

In the novel, open spaces like sidewalks, parks, and public transportation tend to be sites of drama and danger. Alternatively, private and indoor sites depict intimate, domestic life. At the same time, since the turmoil that plagues characters like Leah and Natalie throughout the novel is existential, it is hidden even in private spaces for most of the novel—until it all comes out in the end.

The Pursuit of Authenticity in Modern Life

Every major character in *NW* articulates their version either of what makes life meaningful or of the challenge of pursuing meaning. For some characters, like Michel, the path seems clear: Make money, find a good partner, get a good home, have children, climb the ladder, and enjoy the fruits of a successful life.

For the protagonists Leah and Natalie, however, authenticity is elusive. From childhood on, the two of them struggle to pinpoint who they really are, and what they really want. Most poignantly, their continual awareness of the fact that they don't know the answers to life's questions only increases their anxiety and disaffection. Even after Natalie ostensibly conquers every major aspect of modern urban life—education, career, relationships, family, financial standing—she yearns for something missing. Ambition, many characters discover, adds pressure to the already chaotic world of urban life.

Indeed, *NW* directly demonstrates that ostensible success may not be a path to fulfillment at all. After having children, for instance, Natalie experiences a double-sided sense of guilt, as many contemporary women juggling family and career might. On one hand, she feels anxious about acknowledging her family in her career world, and on the other hand, she feels as though her career takes time, attention, and energy that she should be dedicating to her children.

The Intersection of Identities

NW reflects diversity, ever-present in cosmopolitan London and an increasingly obvious fact of contemporary life. Throughout the novel, different cultures and identities intersect. Residents from a diverse range of cultural backgrounds (Irish, French Algerian, Jamaican, Anglo-Saxon) and socio-economic standings (poor, working-class, and middle-class) live in the same area. Characters experience the collision of cultures in their interactions with each other in this space. Leah and Michel are a mixed-race couple, for instance, and as a child Keisha is fascinated by comparisons between her working-class home and the middle-class Hanwells'.

The intersections are also an irrevocable aspect of personal identity for the characters of *NW*. In some cases, intersections are beyond characters' control. Some of the ways that Frank and Natalie differ, for instance, are attributed to the fact that Frank is mixed-race and born in Italy to a relatively well-off mother, while Natalie's family has Jamaican roots and is decidedly working-class in London. Other identities are acquired through the life choices that characters make. When Natalie decides to pursue college, study law, and accept a job back in London, she must juggle both a new economic identity and the continual reminders of her origins, in addition to trying to negotiate between her multiple identities as a career woman and mother.

At times, characters' identities clash with the realities of life in London, despite the city's diversity. Aside from socio-economic challenges (as when Natalie is said by Nathan and others to have forgotten her roots by becoming financially successful), these conflicts often center on race and nationality. For instance, Leah's mother, Pauline, dismissively refers to Michel as Nigerian—even though he is French Algerian—seeming to equate all of Africa with one nation. Characters like Nathan express frustration with being reduced to their racial identity (he expresses that as a black man, he has been viewed as nothing but a criminal since age 10). Likewise, when Felix is on the train, a pregnant woman asks him to get his "friends" (two other men across the aisle) to free a seat for her, assuming that since they are all black, they must know each other. Throughout the novel, *NW* shows that the pursuit of desired identities, as well as conflicts with given ones, shape characters' sense of self and the struggle to define themselves authentically.

Nature

NW may be a thoroughly urban novel, fixated on London as a cosmopolitan city, but throughout the text, nature and natural imagery provide a subtle but key counterpoint. Characters are periodically drawn to the wildness of nature and the beauty, freedom, and authenticity it represents in contrast to the often grim, inescapable, and chaotic urban landscape.

The novel opens with Leah outdoors, lying in the sun. In "Visitation," as she deals with the aftermath of Shar's theft, her neighbor Ned—a relaxed stoner, one of the few characters in the novel who does not seem crippled by anxiety about his identity—encourages her to enjoy a beautiful sunset. Later, as Michel talks at length about his determination to get ahead in life, Leah finds herself distracted, "thinking of apples" and the blossoms on trees (33). Later, Natalie is also inexplicably attracted to an apple blossom, compelled to snap it off a tree and take it with her on the way to the train, wondering "What could she do with a branch?" (301). Natural imagery like the sunset and apple blossoms serve as islands of fleeting beauty and encapsulate the genuineness that so many of *NW*'s characters seek.

Transportation

Throughout *NW*, modes of transportation—trains and buses, and sometimes cars—signify transformation, escape, and freedom. Given that public transportation is a central aspect of London life and quite literally a means to get from one point to another, this is no surprise. What is particular about the way that *NW* highlights transportation is that it is frequently alluded to in connection to times of significant change in characters' lives.

For example, a flashback section in "Guest" shows that the event that led to Grace and Felix's relationship was a casual meeting at a bus stop. Grace deems the meeting "fate," and ultimately, Felix's relationship with Grace spurs his decision to turn his life around. Ironically, the trip during which Felix is murdered after exiting the train begins with him meeting Tom to buy an MG sports car as a surprise gift for Grace. The optimism of his new life and relationship with her—epitomized by the purchase of a car, a symbol of freedom—is cut short by a tragic murder rooted in a trivial argument on the train.

Modes of transportation are similarly connected to points of change in Keisha/Natalie's life. One day in her youth, Leah decides to take the number 37 bus to see a different set of friends in Camden Lock instead of going to church with Keisha. This bus ride is indicative of the growing separation between the two, as they develop their individual tastes and ambitions in late adolescence. Keisha understands education as a means to escape the confines of Caldwell, yet she is unable to afford the train rides to interview for colleges in Manchester and Edinburgh, and her postsecondary options are limited to Bristol. Nevertheless, college provides an opportunity for her to transform her identity and name.

Transportation enables her and Leah to visit each other at their respective schools, thereby reconnecting on a deeper level. On one of those visits, as Leah gets on the bus to return home, she tells Natalie, "You're the only person I can be all of myself with" (246). As she says goodbye to her friend, Natalie breaks down, gripped by the sense that she cannot articulate her own identity. If the spaces of

London represent what is enduring about their lives, then the modes of transportation that move about those spaces represent characters' struggles with change.

Meals

In *NW,* scenes that involve meals illuminate characters' social interactions and understanding of each other. In some instances, references to meals define differences in class and social standing. When Keisha's father, Gus, treats her and Leah to McDonald's, the girls are delighted; when they run into Pauline Hanwell on the way home, she silently judges them. Keisha, for her part, is infatuated with the way the higher-class Hanwells serve tea, and she imitates this in her own home. Years later, when Michel and Leah are invited to dinners at the home of Natalie and Frank, they feel entirely out of place. Though Leah has been friends with Natalie since childhood, neither she nor Michel "know what to say to barristers and bankers, to the occasional judge. Natalie cannot believe that they are shy. Each time she blames some error of placement but each time the awkwardness remains" (96). In instances like these, meals are an uncomfortable reminder of the class divisions between characters.

At other times, meals are occasions for the novel's perennial questions about identity and authentic selfhood to reemerge. For instance, just prior to Natalie's decision to break up with Rodney and her subsequent fall into ennui about who she really is, she and Leah share a fancy meal on International Women's Day as a chance to be together. Likewise, early in their marriage, Natalie and Frank have brunch with another couple, where the small talk becomes too much for the work-obsessed Natalie, who longs to get up from the restaurant table and "go to the bathroom and spend the next hour alone with her email" (300). These instances of meals in the novel have less to do with class divides; the educated and successful Natalie does not feel uncomfortable at her brunch just as Leah feels uncomfortable at Natalie's dinner parties. Instead, they show that the feelings of insecurity and disaffection so many of *NW*'s characters face emerge no matter who or where they are, and certainly in shared social situations.

1. "'Things change! We're getting there, no?' The woman does not know where there is. She did not know they had set off, nor in which direction the wind is blowing. She does not want to arrive. The truth is she had believed they would be naked in these sheets forever and nothing would come to them ever, nothing but satisfaction. Why must love 'move forward'? Which way is forward?" (Part 1, Page 28)

    The clash between Leah's and Michel's worldviews is as clear as it is drastic. While Michel focuses on advancing materially, economically, and by having children, Leah wonders why they cannot simply live in the present, finding solace in their physical relationship. Michel's language of change, progress, and advancement seems foreign to Leah, ultimately causing her to feel alienated.

2. "Look: you know what is the true difference between these people and me? They don't want to move forward, they don't want to have nothing better than this. But I'm always moving forward, thinking of the next thing." (Part 1, Page 32)

    Michel's ambition and desire do not stem from mere greed or materialism. Instead, the statements he makes about his goals show that his ambition is tied to his understanding of social class. By mentioning differences between those who want to advance and those who do not, and by directly stating that one path is "better," Michel makes clear that he sees ambition as tied to quality of life.

3. "Privately she thinks: you want to be rich like them but you can't be bothered with their morals, whereas I am more interested in their morals than their money, and this thought, this opposition, makes her feel good." (Part 1, Page 90)

Though Leah struggles to find purpose and to understand Michel's ambition, the challenges she faces are deeply connected to the values that she does hold onto. In the supermarket, she realizes that she is bothered by their inability to afford fair trade and local items because she values ethical principles, while Michel is bothered by it because he values economic standing. Throughout the course of the novel, Leah demonstrates a social and ethical consciousness in spite of her existential crisis.

4. "[Barnes] rapped the tree with a knuckle and made Felix stop under it and look up: an enclosing canopy of thick foliage, like standing under the bell skirts of a Disney princess. Felix never knew what to say about nature. He waited. 'A bit of green is very powerful, Felix. Very powerful. 'Specially in England. Even us Londoners born and bred, we need it.'" (Part 2, Page 132)

Barnes is one of the few characters in the novel to make direct reference to the importance of nature. Felix, like Natalie and others, feels thoroughly city-bred and cannot grasp what Barnes means about the power of nature and its necessary contrast to the urban landscape. Ironically, Felix compares the look of the tree to a Disney princess, like the cheap plastic figurines that Grace collects. This reference draws an explicit comparison between manufactured commodities and natural imagery.

5. "Maybe the next cloud overhead would open up and a huge cartoon hand emerge from below, pointing at him, accompanied by a thunderous, authorial voice: TOM MERCER, EPIC FAIL." (Part 2, Page 152)

    Though Tom's appearance in the novel is relatively brief, a passage of stream of consciousness in "Guest" shows that he faces many of the same existential crises as other characters. Despite having an interesting job in marketing, a home, and a girlfriend, Tom is plagued by feelings of inadequacy and a lack of fulfillment. Like Natalie, Leah, and Felix, his parents' judgments also remain a pervasive influence on how he feels about himself and the world.

6. "They were all three familiar to Felix; he'd seen them many times over the years. First her alone; then he moved in. Then the baby turned up, who looked now to be four or five years old. Where had the time gone? Quite often, in good weather, he had watched the woman take pictures of her family on a proper camera set atop a tripod base. 'Oops,' said Annie, 'trouble in paradise.'" (Part 2, Page 174)

    Felix watches a family dine on the rooftop of the building across from Annie's apartment, realizing how time has passed. This passage of time coincided with his years of addiction, and seeing it crystalized in the family underscores the urgency of his desire to turn his life around. The family also represents the ideal of domestic life that he yearns for, and so Annie's sarcastic remark when the woman drops a tray of food emphasizes the contrast between she and Felix.

7. "'You know, Felix'—a dainty little voice, like a waitress reciting the specials—'not everyone wants this

conventional little life you're rowing your boat toward. I like my river of fire. And when it's time for me to go I fully intend to roll off my one-person dinghy into the flames and be consumed. I'm not afraid!'" (Part 2, Page 185)

Most characters in the novel either yearn for something they do not have or struggle to even define what they want from life. Annie, on the other hand, expresses contentment with her way of life. The startling effect of her point of view comes from the ironic fact that the features of her life—drug addiction, a lack of career ambition, disinterest in family or domestic relationships—are vastly different from what other characters long for or represent.

8. "He hurried to the stairs, and was a few steps down when he heard a thud on the carpet above as she went down on her knees, and he knew he was meant to feel heavy, but the truth was he felt like a man undergoing some not-yet-invented process called particle transfer, wonderfully, blissfully light." (Part 2, Page 189)

Felix's motivations for visiting Annie and his final sexual encounter with her are somewhat ambiguous, but the note on which they part leaves no doubt that Felix has changed: While Annie falls, sinking back to her life, he feels reborn. The moment of drama when Annie and Felix argue, first in her apartment and then outside of it, provides a contrast to emphasize just how resolved Felix is to turn his life around.

9. "Felix felt a great wave of approval, smothering and unwanted, directed toward him, and just as surely, contempt and disgust enveloping the two men and

separating them, from Felix, from the rest of the carriage, from humanity." (Part 2, Page 194)

Felix's experience on the train sets his tragic end in motion and illuminates two sides of racism that the novel's characters can face. The white woman who Felix helped on the train mistakenly assumed he was traveling with the other black men on the train, simply because they were of the same race. On the other hand, the other black men (who later mug and stab Felix) see him as weak and contemptible for helping the white woman and for not living up to their view of black male machismo.

10. "'We get into the habit of living before acquiring the habit of thinking,' read Rodney, and then made a note by this sentence: 'So what? (fallacious argument.)'" (Part 3, Page 227)

The very beginning of the relationship between Keisha and Rodney demonstrates how much of it is built around their shared academic and career ambitions. As he diligently studies a book by the philosopher Albert Camus, Rodney reads this quote aloud and makes a note of it. Ironically, he dismisses Camus's point as erroneous, though it encapsulates how Keisha and others devote more time and energy to going through the motions of life than contemplating their sense of purpose.

11. "There seemed no point of entry. The students were tired of things Keisha had never heard of, and horrified by the only thing she knew well: the Bible." (Part 3, Page 235-36)

For several years, much of Keisha's energy has been concentrated on academic achievement and the goal of entering college. Once there, however, she experiences an extraordinary sense of alienation, due to the stark differences in cultural background and socio-economic status between her and other students. This foreshadows later experiences when her achievements in career and family life do not turn out to provide the fulfillment they seemed to promise.

12. "They were going to be lawyers, the first people in either of their families to become professionals. They thought life was a problem that could be solved by means of professionalization." (Part 3, Page 238)

    Confronted by a new-found awareness of class structure and socio-economic divides after beginning college, Rodney and Keisha both set their analytic minds to the task of finding a solution to overcome them. Drawing comparisons between themselves and the people that surround them, they decide that the key to eliminating these divides is career success. While Natalie's later career as a lawyer does provide economic stability, it fails to provide life purpose.

13. "Rodney raised his head from his tort casebook. He had a ruthless look on his face. 'We don't care about trees, Leah,' he said. 'That's your luxury. We haven't got the time to care about trees.'" (Part 3, Page 240)

    Buried in the pile of law books he is studying, Rodney openly rejects Leah's ethical consciousness. The basis of this rejection is rooted in his awareness of class distinctions. He expects that people like he and Keisha, who come from humble economic origins and minority races, must work harder to succeed than someone like

Leah, who is white and from a solid socio-economic background. This situation leaves them, in Rodney's mind, no opportunity to take up causes like Leah's environmental crusade.

14. "Although you may turn up in court armed with reason, we live in an unreasonable world." (Part 3, Page 242)

    One of Natalie's law instructors, Professor Kirkwood, makes this comment in the course of a lesson. For Natalie's character, the comment is less about reason's role in law and order and more about her attempts to control her life. Despite her intelligence, planning, ambition, and outward success, she finds herself running into conflict. Her rationality, in other words, is not enough to hold existential crises at bay.

15. "'Really good to see you,' said Leah. 'You're the only person I can be all of myself with.' Which comment made Natalie begin to cry, not really at the sentiment but rather out of a fearful knowledge that if reversed the statement would be rendered practically meaningless, Ms. Blake having no self to be, not with Leah, or anyone." (Part 3, Page 246)

    Both Leah and Natalie struggle to define themselves, and both are crippled at various points by their own awareness of this struggle. Even when Leah and Natalie are in college, with more opportunities to freely explore and express themselves, Natalie grapples with this problem. This particular crisis of identity, however, closely coincides with major transformations (Keisha's decisions to change her name to Natalie and to break up with Rodney), showing Natalie's tendency to respond to challenges by making resolved choices that feel rational to her.

16. "As one learns very quickly in this profession, fortune favors the brave—but also the pragmatic." (Part 3, Page 284)

Almost as soon as Natalie begins to succeed professionally, she experiences new crises. After facing inappropriate advances from a male lawyer she is working for, Natalie is advised by a senior female lawyer to ignore the issue and focus on opportunities to advance her career. The episode indicates the discrimination that professional women like Natalie deal with and the decisions they consequently face. For Natalie, these sometimes loathsome decisions exacerbate her struggle to navigate her layered roles as a professional, wife, mother, daughter, woman of color, and child of immigrants.

17. "Upon closer inspection the cloud of white separated into thousands of tiny flowers with yellow centers and green bits and pink flecks. A city animal, she did not have the proper name for anything natural." (Part 3, Page 301)

Natalie's entire upbringing has taken place in an urban environment, and she has focused on aspects of urban life such as attaining material stability, becoming educated, and navigating the intersections of multiple identities. However, she feels compelled to pluck an apple blossom from a tree and take it with her as she heads to the train. Inexplicably, the symbol of natural beauty draws her in, suggesting nature's power and the sharp contrast between nature and the built environment of the city.

18. "Daughter drag. Sister drag. Mother drag. Wife drag. Court drag. Rich drag. Poor drag. British drag.

Jamaican drag. Each required a different wardrobe. But when considering these various attitudes she struggled to think what would be the most authentic, or perhaps the least inauthentic." (Part 3, Page 333)

Natalie's catalog of her diverse roles and identities is long and contradictory—she is both rich and poor, and British and foreign, for instance. All of these stick with her, enriching her personality and confusing it. As she moves through the varied spheres of her life, Natalie attempts to alternate her roles and identities as needed. Yet the vast array of them becomes dizzying, and conflicts between them are inevitable, as when she struggles to juggle being both a mother and a barrister.

19. "Walking was what she did now, walking was what she was. She was nothing more or less than the phenomenon of walking. She had no name, no biography, no characteristics." (Part 4, Page 360)

At the moment of her greatest crisis, after Frank discovers her secret affairs, Natalie is at a loss. All of the identities and achievements she bears are shed. Significantly, she takes to the streets when she does not know what else to do, or who she really is. By walking the streets, even aimlessly, Natalie retains the barest sense of being: Thoroughly a Londoner, she can at least blend into the city's landscape.

20. "What you crying for now? You ain't got shit to cry about." (Part 4, Page 377)

Fleeing with Nathan through the streets of their neighborhood, Natalie confronts the people and spaces of her personal history. Nathan—a drug addict, possible pimp, and probable murderer—ostensibly has little room to criticize Natalie's existential woes. On the other hand, because he comes from and continues to inhabit her old neighborhood, humble economic roots, and racial identity, Nathan ironically has the authority to confront Natalie. This confrontation begins a chain of events through which she begins to walk back to some kind of stability.

21. "In the country, if a woman could not face her children, or her friends, or her family—if she were covered in shame—she would probably only need to lay herself down in a field and take her leave by merging, first with the grass underneath her, then with the mulch under that." (Part 4, Page 384)

    As she fleetingly contemplates suicide, standing on a bridge in the midst of cosmopolitan London, Natalie thinks about life outside of the city. Her vision of country life is fanciful and erroneous, but it nevertheless shows that her mind is dwelling on both escaping her personal crises (through suicide) and escaping the city that surrounds her. By reflecting on natural imagery and the country in this moment of crisis, Natalie obliquely demonstrates the powerful effect that the city itself has on her consciousness.

22. "Normally all of her energies would be in defense—she was trained in it—but as she spoke her mind traveled to what felt like open ground, where she was able to almost imagine something like her friend's pain, and in imagining it, recreate some version of it in herself." (Part 5, Page 396)

    Speaking to Michel on the phone, as he frantically seeks help with Leah's nervous breakdown, Natalie snaps out of her own personal drama. She lets down her guard (like the reflexes that stem from being a defense lawyer) and instead simply accepts the privilege of being in the presence of Michel's pain. After she has spent much of the novel in a struggle to define her own identity, the act of laying her self aside to attend to someone else's pain provides a turning point.

23. "The Cock Tavern. MacDonalds. The old Woolworths. The betting shop. The State Empire. Willesden Lane. The cemetery. Whoever said that these were fixed coordinates to which she had to be forever faithful? How could she play them false? Freedom was absolute and everywhere, constantly moving location." (Part 5, Page 397)

    Natalie rattles off a list of familiar sites in the geography of her London neighborhood, describing them like coordinates on the map of her existence. She draws a contrast between these sites, which seem fixed in both time and space, and the constant movement of life. While she rejects the sites as fixed and confining, the fact is that she has chosen to remain in London. The conflicts she faces are rooted in a struggle to find an authentic way to inhabit this space rather than in the space itself.

24. "If candor were a thing in the world that a person could hold and retain, if it were an object, maybe Natalie Blake would have seen that the perfect gift at this moment was an honest account of her own difficulties and ambivalences, clearly stated, without disguise, embellishment or prettification. But Natalie Blake's instinct for self-defense, for self-preservation, was simply too strong." (Part 5, Page 399)

Though broken down by her domestic drama with Frank and the shock of Leah's mental health crisis, Natalie nevertheless holds on to the self-control that she has trusted when making decisions throughout her life. Instead of empathetically discussing her own struggles and crises with Leah, Natalie suggests that her friend remember what is good in her life. Even at this late stage in the novel, Natalie is propelled more by rational choice than emotion, in spite of the problems doing so has sometimes created.

25. "'I just don't understand why I have this life,' she said, quietly." (Part 5, Page 399)

Leah's remark is one of the most plaintive in the novel, capturing a distinct aspect of the existential crisis that many characters face. In the diverse Caldwell and the sprawling city of London beyond, it is hard for many of them to feel as though they are unique and that they can construct an authentic sense of self. When Leah thinks about characters like Shar and Felix, she wonders about why they received their fates and about how easily she could have taken their place. While Natalie suggests that they made conscious choices to lead better lives, Leah's perspective provides an alternative perspective worth consideration.

ESSAY TOPICS

1. Both Natalie and Leah seek something when they feel unfulfilled in their lives: Natalie pursues casual sex with strangers, while Leah becomes fixated on tracking down and helping Shar. What is similar about the causes of their obsessions? What is different about them?

2. Choose one of *NW*'s minor characters, like Ned, Barnes, or Pauline. Explore their significance in the novel. How do they exemplify or provide contrast to *NW*'s major themes?

3. Several characters in *NW,* from Marcia to Michel, view education and career as keys to success in life, yet their reasons for doing so aren't uniform. Discuss the differences between their perspectives, and how those differences motivate characters' actions.

4. *NW* 's characters share common concerns stemming from the realities of London life: multiculturalism, the intersection of multiple identities, the pursuit of economic success, family drama, and the search for personal fulfillment, among others. Some characters respond to these concerns with optimism, while others feel themselves lost in the chaos. Would you defend one group or the other? Or would you reconcile the two positions?

5. Racial tensions in contemporary London are reflected throughout *NW.* In what ways do these tensions highlight characters' senses of identity? In what ways do they highlight their struggle to create an authentic sense of self?

6. Feminist concerns, and general questions of what it means to be a modern woman, surface throughout *NW*. Discuss these concerns by comparing the perspectives of Leah and Natalie to the worldviews of their mothers, Pauline and Marcia.

7. Undoubtedly, *NW* focuses on city life, but references to nature and natural imagery punctuate the narrative. What is the significance of these references for the existential issues the characters face?

8. *NW* features numerous passages that make direct reference to London geography, including map directions, names of neighborhoods, streets, buildings, and parks, and detailed descriptions of characters' walking paths through the city. Why do you think Smith focused so much on providing authentic geographic details? What effect do you think they have on the narrative?

9. Discuss the significance of *NW*'s non-linear narrative—its jumps in time, side stories, and multiple converging plots. What is the effect of this unusual narrative structure? How does it relate to the novel's core themes?

10. In what ways do you think *NW*'s experimental style contributes to the presentation of its key themes?

CPSIA information can be obtained
at www.ICGtesting.com
Printed in the USA
BVHW031340051222
653478BV00016B/143

9 798615 499999